D1647931

Catholic Schools and the Law

A Teacher's Guide

[Second Edition]

**Also by Mary Angela Shaughnessy
published by Paulist Press**

Ministry and the Law: What You Need to Know

Catholic Schools and the Law

A Teacher's Guide

[Second Edition]

Mary Angela Shaughnessy, S.C.N., J.D.

PAULIST PRESS
New York/Mahwah, New Jersey

377.82
S S33

Cover design by Lynn Else and Valerie L. Petro

Copyright © 2000 by Mary Angela Shaughnessy

All rights reserved. No part of this book may be reproduced or transmitted in any form or by any means, electronic or mechanical, including photocopying, recording or by any information storage and retrieval system without permission in writing from the Publisher.

ISBN: 0-8091-3964-2

Published by Paulist Press
997 Macarthur Boulevard
Mahwah, New Jersey 07430

www.paulistpress.com

Printed and bound in the
United States of America

Contents

Chapter One
Why You Need to Know   1

Chapter Two
How Much Do You Know?   5

Chapter Three
What Laws Affect Catholic Schools?   24

Chapter Four
Why Lawsuits Happen and How to Avoid Them   36

Chapter Five
The Faculty Handbook: Part of Your Contract   53

Chapter Six
Selected Issues   62

Glossary of Terms   71

Bibliography   73

I dedicate this text, with love and gratitude, to my brothers—

Thomas Michael Shaughnessy
Edward Michael Shaughnessy III (1953–1999)
Lawrence Michael Shaughnessy

and my sisters—

Janet Shaughnessy Kellogg
Karen Shaughnessy Schultz

who shared Catholic school education and family life with me.

No one could ask for better brothers and sisters.

Acknowledgments

I want to thank all those who have a part in the development of this work. First, I express my gratitude to the Paulist Press and to Maria Maggi, now managing editor, for publishing this revised edition of *Catholic Schools and the Law: A Teacher's Guide*. Without their support, this book would not have been possible.

It has been my privilege to minister in the field of Catholic education for almost thirty years, not counting my sixteen years of elementary, secondary, and undergraduate education. My work as a professor, lecturer, and writer has allowed me to meet many committed Catholic educators, and I am grateful. In particular, I thank my present and former students who truly teach me more than I believe I teach them.

My religious community, the Sisters of Charity of Nazareth, supports my work in the field of Catholic schools and the law. Our shared life as sisters is an integral part of my life. I also thank my religious sister, Miriam Corcoran, S.C.N., who has provided valuable editorial assistance for this work and all my works.

My colleagues at Spalding University, where I am privileged to minister, offer much support. Most especially, I thank Dr. Thomas Oates, Spalding University president, who is a true advocate for Catholic education and who allows me the freedom to teach, practice law, write, and lecture across the country. Without his support, I would find it very difficult to fulfill this ministry.

Lastly, I thank you, the readers. May God bless you in your ministry of Catholic education.

—*Mary Angela Shaughnessy, S.C.N., J.D., Ph.D.*

CHAPTER ONE

Why You Need to Know

Catholic school teachers of the third millennium have more legal concerns than the teachers of any other era ever experienced. Student violence has rocked any sense of security educators might once have had. Important issues of today, such as violence, confidentiality, sexual harassment, and others, were rarely, if ever, discussed. Now, ten years after the publication of the first edition of this text, these topics demand primary attention.

In 1990 the first edition of this text began with the following paragraph:

> The years since 1960 have been times of rapid change in all areas of American society. The Catholic Church has not been immune to change. The Second Vatican Council ushered in a new era of lay participation and involvement in the church. Holding fast to age-old teachings, church documents such as *To Teach As Jesus Did*, nonetheless mandated new directions for the ministry of teaching. In less than thirty years the majority of teachers in Catholic schools has shifted from members of religious congregations to members of the laity. Clearly, the future of Catholic education in the United States depends upon the continued dedication of lay teachers and administrators.

1

Educators who enter the third millennium know that change contin-ues, seemingly unchecked. The Catholic bishops of the United States, collectively and individually, issue educational documents that both instruct and challenge. Members of religious orders and priests consti-tute less than 15 percent of the staff members in Catholic schools, and the percentage of their representation among administrators is even lower. Most Catholic schools are now directed by lay persons. The min-istry of Catholic education, then, depends on the faithfulness and com-petencies of its lay teachers and administrators. Knowledge of school law and the ability to apply that law are two of these necessary competencies.

Prior to 1960, lawsuits against public, let alone private, elementary and secondary schools were relatively rare. Those few cases brought against private schools primarily involved higher education. Courts were extremely reluctant to rule against schools, administrators, and staff members. Practicing the doctrine of judicial restraint and sub-scribing to the theory of in loco parentis—that is, the school acts in the place of parents—courts recognized schools as having almost unlimited authority.

The 1961 landmark case *Dixon v. Alabama*, involving African-American college students suspended for participating in a lunch counter sit-in as a protest to laws that did not allow them to eat in the same places where white people ate, broke the court's restraint and won constitutional due process protections for public college and uni-versity students. By 1969, public secondary teachers and students had firmly established their rights through such rulings as those found in *Tinker v. Des Moines Independent School District.* Perhaps the most famous quote in all of school law is the following found here: "It can hardly be argued that either teachers or students shed their Constitutional rights at the [public] school house gate." Catholic and other private schools were not included in the ruling.

Since the 1970s a fairly large body of statutory and case law is avail-able to guide public school decision making. It was only in the late 1980s and 1990s that the study of Catholic schools and civil law emerged as a separate field of inquiry. The 1980s witnessed a rise in the number of cases brought by private school teachers and students against schools and administrators. The reticence that once seemed to preclude a church member's suing a church authority largely disappeared. The doctrine of separation of state, which had protected church-sponsored schools from being successfully sued, was set aside unless the issue at hand was clearly doctrinal, in which case, the court would practice judicial restraint and refuse to rule on the case.

Parents, students, and teachers continue to sue Catholic and other private schools. Unless there is a clear reason for judicial restraint today, courts will hear cases involving Catholic schools and their staff and students. It should be noted that, as of the date of this text, the United States Supreme Court has never agreed to review a case involving private elementary and secondary school discipline of students. To the best of this writer's knowledge, only one case involving a teacher was heard by the Supreme Court, the 1982 *Rendell-Baker v. Kohn* case, involving a private, nonsectarian school, and the court ruled in favor of the private school. It appears that the Supreme Court is somewhat reluctant to intervene in the nonpublic sector. That reluctance may be diminishing as the numbers of Catholic school cases increase in both state and federal courts.

Although the myth is receding, some teachers still believe that persons won't sue them or their Catholic school or parish. If such a statement were ever true, it is certainly not true today. Although lawsuits against the Catholic Church rarely occurred in the 1960s and only occasionally in the 1970s, the next two decades witnessed a near explosion of cases. It should be noted that sexual abuse cases involving Catholic school/parish personnel represent only a small percentage of lawsuits filed against the Catholic Church. The vast majority of Catholic school cases allege negligence.

Some educators may still espouse the theory, "What you don't know can't hurt you," but ignorance of the law is no defense in a court of law. Each teacher must understand the basics of school law, a tool that can save a person from aggravation in day-to-day professional living and, in the worst-case scenario, from an expensive lawsuit.

Knowledge of school law is, of course, not the most important part of Catholic education, but the law creates a parameter inside which Catholic schools and personnel operate. If individuals move outside that parameter, they may lose the ministry inside the parameter.

The purpose of this text is threefold: to provide Catholic school teachers with an instrument by which to assess their knowledge of school law; to offer a practical guide to the principles of school law; and to offer specific recommendations for teachers. Those who are interested in reading the cases named in this and the following chapters may consult the bibliography for appropriate citations.

The following pretest is an assessment of one's current knowledge of school law. The results of this assessment, coupled with appropriate in-service training and reading, can help teachers both to raise their levels of awareness of legal matters and to avoid legal problems.

CHAPTER TWO

How Much Do You Know?

Legal Pretest for Educators in Catholic Schools

✎ *Please answer* **True** *or* **False.**

_____ 1. Students and teachers in private schools have the same rights that students and teachers in public schools have.

_____ 2. It is never legally permissible to leave students unattended in a classroom or while waiting to participate in any school activity.

_____ 3. A student can never be expelled and a teacher can never be dismissed for a single action.

_____ 4. If two students begin to fight and the teacher cannot stop the fight, he or she should leave the students and summon help as quickly as possible.

_____ 5. Emotional abuse can be considered child abuse.

_____ 6. Courts will protect the confidentiality of student/ teacher communications.

_____ 7. Teachers and administrators can be held liable for the actions of a student who attacks, injures, and/or kills others.

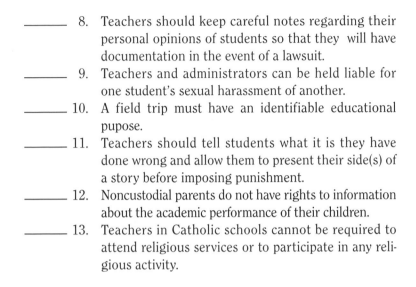

_____ 8. Teachers should keep careful notes regarding their personal opinions of students so that they will have documentation in the event of a lawsuit.

_____ 9. Teachers and administrators can be held liable for one student's sexual harassment of another.

_____ 10. A field trip must have an identifiable educational pupose.

_____ 11. Teachers should tell students what it is they have done wrong and allow them to present their side(s) of a story before imposing punishment.

_____ 12. Noncustodial parents do not have rights to information about the academic performance of their children.

_____ 13. Teachers in Catholic schools cannot be required to attend religious services or to participate in any religious activity.

Answers and Commentary

1. *False. Students and teachers in private schools have the same rights that students and teachers in public schools have.*

This statement, although many members of the public probably do not realize it, is false. Students and teachers in public schools have constitutional, contractual, statutory, and common law rights. Those in private schools do not have constitutional rights. Some examples will illustrate.

A student who comes to school wearing a button such as, "Abortion is a woman's right," "Legalize assisted suicide now," or even "Ordain women now" would most likely be told to remove the button. Catholic school officials would be well within their rights to require that the mandates of the Catholic Church are followed and that no one take a stand opposed to church teachings. In a public school a principal could not exercise such control because of the First Amendment right to freedom of expression.

The *Tinker* case mentioned in chapter 1 delineated the boundaries of symbolic speech in the public school. *Tinker* involved students who wore black armbands to protest the Vietnam War. The principals of their respective schools had forbidden the wearing of such armbands and threatened dissenters with suspension. Students who refused to remove the armbands were suspended and told they could not return to school until they complied with the ban on the wearing of armbands. *Tinker* diminished the authority of school officials and held that persons in public schools do have constitutional protections that must be guaranteed.

Constitutional freedoms are guaranteed by the government and its agencies, and a public school is a governmental agency. Therefore, a public school must protect the constitutional rights of students. However, the Catholic school is a private, not a state, agency. Thus, its officials are under no governmental requirement to grant constitutional protections to its students. A Catholic school may well model its disciplinary code on certain basic freedoms, but unless officials want to surrender control and be recognized as state agents without any of the benefits of state agents, school officials should guard against using the words *constitutional freedoms* in its documents. If a Catholic school chooses to grant constitutional freedoms to its students, it will be bound by its decision—not because of the requirements of the Constitution, but because of the requirements of contract law.

Similarly, the public school teacher has a whole panoply of guaranteed constitutional protections that are not provided to the Catholic school teacher. Catholic school teachers, like their students, do not have constitutional rights that the Catholic school must protect. Catholic school teachers can be subject to behavior codes and speech restrictions that could not be enforced in public schools. Catholic school teachers may also be forbidden to criticize the Catholic Church and/or its teachings to their students.

At first glance, these restrictions may seem unfair; yet a similar price is paid by anyone who works in a private institution. If a person works at a fast-food establishment, the person will probably be required to wear a uniform and will most certainly not be allowed to wear buttons advertising a different fast-food establishment.

The bottom line is that when one enters a private institution, one voluntarily surrenders the protections of the Constitution. A Catholic school teacher or student can always leave the Catholic school, but, so long as the person remains in the institution, constitutional protections are not available. Thus, the Catholic school does not have to accept behaviors that the public school has no choice but to accept.

2. False. It is never legally permissible to leave students unattended in a classroom or while waiting to participate in any school activity.

There are occasions when it is legally permissible to leave students unattended in a classroom. Well-meaning principals may tell teachers and other staff members that, legally, students can never be left unattended, but there are occasions when students legally can be left without adult supervision. One such occasion is the need for the adult supervisor to use a restroom. The other such occasion is some legitimate emergency.

The "test" for liability for injuries occurring during a teacher's absence will always be, "Did the adult act as a reasonable person would be expected to act?" Courts talk about a seemingly mythical creature, a reasonable person. In other words, would the average teacher, in similar circumstances, act the way this teacher acted? It is reasonable that an adult spend five minutes in a restroom. The key word is *reasonable*. It is not reasonable to be absent from a classroom for a half-hour under normal circumstances. Teachers must guard against extending restroom breaks to include making phone calls, using the copy machine, or taking coffee breaks.

Emergencies are practically impossible to define. Anyone who has worked with children and/or adolescents knows that things can happen that could never be foreseen. The important consideration will be, "Did the adult act reasonably?" Common sense and ordinary prudence are good guides in these situations.

This second statement could be reworded to make it true by writing, "It is never legally permissible to leave students *without direction* in a classroom." Teachers and other supervising adults should have procedures to be followed when the teacher is not present, and students should know those procedures. Teachers should periodically review all rules for classroom procedures, particularly those involving behavior when the teacher is physically absent from the classroom or learning area. At the very least, students should be required to remain in their seats and behave as they are expected to act when the teacher is present.

The legal principle involved here is, "The younger the child chronologically or mentally, the greater the standard of care." This principle means that one can leave eighth graders and high schoolers alone, and they are more likely to do what they are told than first graders would be. It seems to this writer, at least, that the architects of this principle have probably never taught in a classroom. Most teachers would agree that first graders are more likely to stay in their seats and do as they are told than are eighth graders or high school students. In any event, however, teachers are held to a higher standard of care for younger children than they are for older children. Eighth graders could probably be allowed to tour a museum or library without the presence of an adult at all times; first graders certainly could not. The important question to bear in mind is, "Are my actions those of a reasonable person?" Teachers whose students are kindergarten age and younger are obviously held to a much higher standard than are teachers of older students.

Extracurricular activities and athletics pose special supervisory problems. It is not legally acceptable to have students waiting for such activities to begin or for a ride at the end without adult supervision. One way to avoid the problems presented by parents who drop off students early for practices and fail to reclaim them in a timely manner is to enforce a rule that states, "On the second (or third) time a student arrives before supervision is present or remains on the grounds more than a half-hour after the activity, the student is dropped from the activity." Supervisors and administrators must be committed to enforcing the rule, even if it means dropping the lead in the musical, the editor of the yearbook, or the football captain. There are, of course, other less severe measures that could be considered. The important reality is *do something.* Do not take refuge in the belief that because nothing has ever happened in this school, nothing ever will. The unsupervised presence of students before and after school as they wait for activities to begin or for pickup at activities' end is one of the biggest lawsuits waiting to happen in most schools.

In summary, no teacher is required to be physically present at all times; courts do understand that accidents and other emergencies can occur. Courts, however, do expect that teachers will have prepared students for their possible absence through the development and implementation of classroom rules for behavior.

3. *False. A student can never be expelled and a teacher can never be dismissed for a single action.*

Students *can* be expelled and teachers *can* be dismissed for single actions. Some behavior is so reprehensible that it cannot be tolerated in Catholic schools or other institutions. The law will support an official who dismisses an individual for inappropriate behavior so long as the dismissal can be supported by the written policies and procedures of the school.

The problem that presents itself is, "What should an administrator do when the teacher or student has only been accused?" The U.S. system of justice is grounded in the principle of "innocent until proven guilty." Inappropriate behavior allegations are usually made before the accused is found guilty or innocent in a court of law or admits the truth of the allegation. Although one can certainly argue that it often seems as if U.S. justice really operates in practice on the principle of "guilty until proven innocent," the presumption of innocence is sacred. Policies and procedures for dealing with such situations should be clear and understandable.

First, administrators must understand that they cannot think of every possible wrong that a student or teacher might commit. It is better to have at least some general parameters for behavior than to attempt to list everything a person might do. In a student discipline case, *Geraci v. St. Xavier High School,* the student handbook prohibited "conduct detrimental to the reputation of the school." The statement could be strengthened by adding, "conduct, *whether inside or outside school, that is detrimental to the reputation of the school.*" Such a clause avoids the necessity for long lists of offenses.

Because allegations can be made and denied, administrators should have a process in place for dealing with them as expeditiously as possible. The following policies are suggestions:

a student accused of a serious wrong can be placed on a home study program

and

a teacher accused of a serious wrong can be placed on administrative leave pending the outcome of an investigation or adjudication.

All arrests do not lead to convictions. The lack of a conviction may not mean that the behavior never occurred; it may mean that the jury did not find "beyond a reasonable doubt" that the behavior occurred. Students are often placed in diversionary or rehabilitative programs or in community service, rather than being convicted of misdemeanors and felonies. The criminal records of most juveniles are sealed, and school officials may find it next to impossible to determine what ruling a judge or jury made. Some adult first-time offenders are also placed in diversion and/or community service. In such cases, the school official will have to rely on the results of an internal investigation.

Some investigations or processes may already be in place and, if so, should be followed; for example, virtually every diocese has a sexual abuse policy that prohibits persons from taking actions not in accordance with the policy. Administrators and teachers must be sure that they adhere to the steps in official policy. In the majority of such cases, the official receiving the allegation notifies diocesan authorities and then follows their direction. Very often, the problem of the presence of the accused in sexual abuse cases is eliminated because the vast majority of policies require immediate suspension from duties on the receipt of a credible accusation. Accused employees and concerned administrators may ask whether the leave of absence is paid or unpaid. It seems only appropriate that persons be paid, if at all possible. If it is impossible to pay them, administrators must understand that the school will be liable for back pay and interest if the individual is neither convicted nor otherwise determined to be guilty of the charged offense.

Teachers may question the wisdom of students being placed on home study programs because the classroom teachers bear the burden of preparing and evaluating work for the students. Although it is true that such arrangements can be time consuming, it is crucial that persons whose guilt has not been established be treated as fairly as possible. Home study programs serve as a vehicle for fair treatment.

4. *False. If two students begin to fight and the teacher cannot stop the fight, he or she should leave the students and summon help as quickly as possible.*

No matter how dangerous the fight seems to be with the teacher present, it is generally conceded that the situation will worsen if the teacher leaves. A reasonable person would send another student to get help from an administrator or other teacher. If no one is nearby, a teacher could attempt to get a passerby to go for help or could shout loudly to attract attention. Teachers should leave fighting students only after all other options have been exhausted.

When discussing fight prevention and intervention, it is important to understand that women have much more leeway than men in their behavior. Many women educators can recount stories of breaking up fights between boys by simply moving between the boys, placing a hand on each boy's chest and separating them. If a man were to employ that technique with two girls, he might face allegations of sexual harassment. Although such allegations might be false, he would still have to answer the accusations. Sometimes, despite an educator's best efforts, he is accused of sexual harassment and/or abuse.

To prevent such situations, all teachers, male and female, should commit themselves to avoiding even the appearance of impropriety. More than twenty years ago, this author recalls a male teacher telling her that he "would never stay alone in a room with a girl unless the door was opened or a window permitted some observation of the room." Today this is good advice for everyone, regardless of the gender of teacher or student. It is indeed sad when reputations and careers are damaged that could easily have been saved by prudent forethought. All teachers need to reflect on situations they have encountered or may encounter and attempt to construct coping strategies before they are ever needed.

5. *True. Emotional abuse can be considered child abuse.*
The reporting of emotional abuse as child abuse is a relatively recent phenomenon. Prior to the mid 1990s, police and social service agencies rarely investigated claims of emotional abuse. Today, however, emotional abuse is considered a type of child abuse that must be investigated.

Child-abuse reporting laws require that all abuse be reported; it is the responsibility of the agency receiving the report, not the person making the report, to determine the truth of the matter. It is becoming more and more common for parents, students, and even other teachers to report teachers for emotional abuse of children. Emotional abuse is not synonymous with losing one's temper or reprimanding students. Rather, emotional abuse demeans a student or students for no good reason. A teacher who says, "Johnny, you can do better than a *D*" is not abusive, but one who says, "I should know better than to expect anything better than a *D* from you because you're stupid" may be considered abusive. All educators need to examine carefully their own patterns of behavior and to correct any that might possibly be construed as abusive, first, of course, for the good of the pupils and, second, to avoid liability for injury.

6. *False. Courts will protect the confidentiality of student/teacher communications.*

For years, many Catholic educators, like most other educators, believed that student/teacher communications were sacred. Teachers routinely told students that they would not repeat what students told them or report what students wrote in journals or other assignments. When tragedies occurred, even if students had given teachers some inclination of their destructive tendencies, no one considered suing the school or the teacher. Today the opposite reality is present.

Teachers cannot afford to think that they can help all students all the time, for such a task is impossible. If a student, laboring for breath, came to a teacher, the teacher would quickly obtain medical assistance and notify the student's parents. Yet, emotional problems are no less real than physical ones, and the teacher who deals with such problems unaided may well be courting tragedy for both self and student.

Confidentiality is generally considered to mean that one individual will keep private information confided by another and will not reveal that information to a third party. Friends and family members share confidences with each other. One individual may say to another, "This is confidential; you cannot repeat it." The person offering the confidence generally has a right to expect that the person receiving the confidence will keep the matter secret. But there are recognized limits to what family and friends will keep private. If one's friend confides that she has purchased a gun and intends to kill her family and herself, the individual hearing that has moral as well as legal obligations to intervene.

Nonetheless, it is common to hear of an adult who would not hesitate to get help for a friend to believe that a student who is talking about suicide is not serious, can be talked out of the behavior, or is incapable of carrying out the promised behavior. Psychologists and other health care professionals report that young people often cannot and do not think through the long-term ramifications of suicide or homicide. A large number of young people continue to be fascinated with death and with famous people who died young.

If a student tells a teacher that he or she is going to harm self or others, the teacher must reveal that information, even if a promise of confidentiality has been given. In a number of lawsuits brought against teachers and school districts, parents sought damages from teachers who had been entrusted with their children's confidences but did not notify anyone about potential dangers. The 1995 case of *Brooks v. Logan School District* is one such case.

In *Brooks* the parents of a student who committed suicide filed a wrongful death action and a claim for negligent infliction of emotional distress against a teacher who required students to keep a journal as part of an English class. The student faithfully recorded entries for the four months prior to his successful suicide. After his death, the journal was given to his parents. The student's writing indicated possible mental disturbance and a fascination with the macabre; he seemed to be mesmerized by the writings of Edgar Allan Poe. One entry read:

> Well, Edgar Allan Poe, I can live with studying that stuff he wrote, especially the one short story about the evil eye... I used to write poems until I pronounced myself dead in one of them and how I could [sic] write poems or stories if I was dead... Recently, see I went into a medium of depression and wrote poems about two special people... I told them it was too bad that I had to say goodby this way like that, but it would be the only way and I felt better... (p. 81)

The teacher maintained that she did not read student entries but merely checked for dates and lengths of entries. The parents alleged that the teacher told them she had "reread" the entries, which would imply, of course, an initial reading when submitted. The teacher denied making the statement.

Nonetheless, the appellate court reversed a lower court's ruling of summary judgment in favor of the teacher and the school district and held that there were issues of fact that could only be determined in a trial. Thus, the lower court was expected to determine that, if the student's suicide were foreseeable, a reasonable teacher would have recognized the possibility of suicide and notified someone. Significantly, the court made analogies between the *Brooks* case and those cases in which jailers have been found liable for the suicide of prisoners who had exhibited warning signs that went unheeded.

Thus, it is a myth that teachers, counselors, mental health professionals, social workers, and others have legal immunity from responsibility for injuries that may arise from their not acting on confidential information they receive. Virtually every state has abolished counselor immunity. A counselor or teacher to whom a student discloses plans to kill self or others and takes no action will not be able legally to decline to answer questions under oath, nor will the educator be held blameless for injury and/or death.

A teacher, therefore, must assume that no legal protection exists for those who receive student confidences. A teacher who wants to be approachable and helpful as well as be a good subject matter teacher must state and implement the rules for confidentiality before confidences are received. Teachers should instruct students, "I will keep your confidences so long as no one's life, health, or safety is involved. If life, health, or safety is involved, I must reveal what you tell me, and you need to know that I will."

Student journals often contain warning signs. Teachers who assign journals or any other written assignment must understand that they are expected to *read* what is written. One person observed, "If you don't have time to read it, don't assign it." Teachers must read what students write and submit.

Perhaps the best question to ask when struggling with issues of confidentiality is, "If my child had written or said this, would I expect someone to tell me?"

7. *True. Teachers and administrators can be held liable for the actions of a student who attacks, injures, and/or kills another.*

The issue discussed in question number 6 above is at the heart of the truth of this statement; it is, nonetheless, a larger question than simple confidentiality. Students and teachers can display behaviors that should be viewed as warning signals without ever explicitly saying that they intend to do harm. The epidemic of student violence that began toward the end of the last decade spawned a series of lawsuits filed by parents whose children had been killed or injured by other students while at school.

The parents of the victims of the Heath High School, Paducah, Kentucky, shootings filed a civil action in McCracken Circuit Court of Kentucky against the perpetrator's parents, teachers, friends, and local officials for negligence in failing to heed warning signals, respond appropriately, and warn possible victims. For informational purposes, some allegations contained in the complaint follow:

26. Defendants [friends of the perpetrator]...conspired with Michael Carneal to take over Heath High School and murder faculty and students, including the Plaintiffs' decedents.

27. [Defendant students] were aware that Michael Carneal had brought guns to school prior to the shootings. They did nothing to alert officials.

28. Defendant [student] failed to properly secure his weapons, which were used [in the murder.]

29. Defendant [student] bought a pistol from Michael Carneal approximately two months before the shootings. He knew that Carneal did not own the pistol, but it instead was owned by [the perpetrator's father]. He nonetheless resold it to [another student]. He told no one in authority about the weapon.

30. Defendant school board, administrators, and employees failed to implement any security measures that would have prevented the deaths of [decedents], failed to take any action on the many warning signals given by Michael Carneal prior to the shootings, and failed to intercept Michael Carneal on the day of the shootings.

These claims appear to depend heavily on the perpetrator's writings, which included a piece called "Halloween Surprise" that described shooting students and detonating an atomic bomb at the school, as well as presenting impaled students to his mother as a gift. Other warning signals cited in the complaint are: Carneal's use of computers and the Internet; various statements; various stealing episodes; posters and other items dealing with death; prior instances of bringing guns and weapons to school. Teachers are alleged liable because

84. Defendant teachers failed to notify either school officials or John and Ann Carneal that Michael Carneal was writing extremely violent and gruesome stories for class assignments that dealt with the death of classmates and the taking over of the school by force. Such intervention and notification would have prevented the deaths of the Plaintiffs' decedents. They also failed to take any action on Carneal's many disciplinary problems.

As newspapers often warn readers, claims made in a case represent only one side of the case. The purpose of including some excerpts from this complaint is to indicate potential areas of teacher liability for student violence. The best practice for all teachers is to report everything that causes them concern. Student violence is one area where overreaction is better than underreaction.

8. *False. Teachers should keep careful notes regarding their personal opinions of students so that they will have documentation in the event of a lawsuit.*
The difficulty in this statement lies in the words *personal opinions.* One's personal opinions do not constitute a good basis for making judgments about a student. *Professional opinions,* supported by documented evidence, count.

Teachers are best advised not to make any unnecessary oral or written comments about students. "I feel that this student is a trouble-maker," for example, is subjective; any statement that becomes part of a student's record should meet the following three criteria:

- the statement should be specific;
- the statement should be behavioral in its orientation; and
- the statement should be verifiable.

For example, the statement, "Johnny's highest grade on a mathematics test was 65 percent" is specific, behaviorally oriented, and verifiable. The statement, "Johnny has no aptitude for arithmetic" is too vague, doesn't state the behavioral basis for the statement, and would probably be difficult to verify.

Teachers may rightfully ask what they are to do when a student has problems and they are asked to give written evaluations of the student's behavior and/or academic progress. Keeping in mind the three principles stated above should prove helpful. No one would suggest that teachers give evaluations and/or recommendations that are patently untrue nor that situations causing concern should be allowed to go unreported.

The important consideration in any reporting, oral or written, concerning students, is objectivity. There is no room for subjectivity in any student reporting, although, as human beings, teachers may find it hard to avoid subjectivity. Keeping remarks focused on behavior that is specific, behaviorally oriented, and verifiable is crucial. These topics will be treated in greater detail later in this text.

9. *True. Teachers and administrators can be held liable for one student's sexual harassment of another.*

The last decade of the twentieth century witnessed an alarming increase in allegations of student sexual harassment of other students. No longer is sexual harassment considered something that is found only between two adults or between an adult and a child. School children and adolescents claim that peers have harassed them. Administrators, teachers, pastors, and board members may be uncertain as to the best approach to dealing with these problems.

First, administrators and board members must ensure that sexual harassment policies of the school, parish, and/or diocese are in place and understood by all affected. Teachers and others may need some education in the definition of sexual harassment, prevention of it, and response to it. Every comment made concerning gender is not, for example, sexual harassment. A male student who says, "Boys, not girls, are supposed to be class president" may not be guilty of sexual harassment but may be guilty of a new tort recognized in some states as gender harassment; the prohibition of gender harassment has not been universally adopted in the United States.

Teachers and principals must take a zero tolerance stance with regard to sexual harassment. Excuses such as "I was only joking" should not be accepted. In some cases that have reached the courts, teachers and/or administrators have told female students, "Boys will be boys." The Catholic Church teaches that all persons are equally valuable in God's eyes; therefore, the equality of all must be protected in the Catholic school.

10. *True. A field trip must have an identifiable educational purpose.*
Today's courts are concerned with the *why* of field trips. As cases cited later in this text will illustrate, it is imperative that school officials be able to cite solid educational reasons for taking a field trip. Parents send their children to Catholic school for an education; if students take off-campus trips, teachers should be able to articulate how *what* they are doing relates to the original purpose for which the parents sent the children to school. Later discussion will include pertinent case law.

Teachers should choose field trips that have readily apparent educational purposes. Eighth grade "rites of passage" trips to amusement parks, for example, generally will not fall into the category of educational trips. However, some amusement park administrators have developed lesson plans for teachers to use in the park setting. So long as a teacher prepares for and implements an educationally sound plan, there should be no legal problems from the standpoint of educational purpose.

Teachers should consider writing a cover letter to include with permission slips. The cover letter should clearly explain the educational purposes of the trip. In the alternative, the educational purpose could be noted on the permission slip. Parents should be given information indicating that the field trip is an extension of the classroom learning experience.

Such an approach makes good educational sense, but it also makes good legal sense. In the unfortunate case in which a student is injured, a school will be in a much better legal position if the educational value of the trip is clearly evident; however, the school will probably find it difficult to justify a trip that was taken purely for enjoyment.

11. *True. Teachers should tell students what it is they have done wrong and allow them to present their side(s) of a story before imposing punishment.*

Although there is no legal requirement that Catholic school teachers must follow all nine elements of procedural due process: (1) notice and (2) a hearing before (3) an impartial tribunal that allows (4) confrontation with accusers, (5) opportunity to cross-examine, (6) the opportunity to call one's own witnesses, (7) the right to have an attorney present, (8) the right to have a transcript of the proceedings, and (9) the right to appeal, Catholic educators are still expected to observe the covenant of good faith and fair dealing in their interactions with others. Courts can and do require that all persons, including those in the private sector, meet at least the first three requirements so that fairness can be met.

The truth of the statement may appear obvious to many readers. However, the practice of taking time to listen to a student's story may not always be observed, particularly if the teacher has just observed a student committing the infraction. It may seem like a waste of time to let a student tell the teacher that what the teacher saw was not what occurred. However, every teacher reading this text has probably, on at least one occasion, been absolutely convinced that a student did something that it was later proven he or she did not do. Beyond that reality, most people can recall times when teachers accused them of doing something that they did not do. Many people cannot remember the names of all their teachers, but they can often describe a false accusation as though it were made yesterday.

A teacher who truly wishes to witness to both basic fairness and gospel values should take the time necessary to give students the opportunity to explain behavior. Mistakes can still be made, of course, but the teacher will have demonstrated a willingness to listen.

12. False. Noncustodial parents do not have rights to information about the academic performance of their children.

Simply losing physical custody of a child does not render a noncustodial parent less than a parent. Unless there is a court order to the contrary, noncustodial parents have the right to talk with school personnel, to receive unofficial copies of records, and to receive school mailings (for which a reasonable fee may be charged). Many custodial parents are not aware of the laws protecting the rights of noncustodial parents and may demand that the school provide no information or access to noncustodial parents. School administrators may have to decline such demands if there is no documentation to support the demands. Teachers should also be aware of custody law and of the special circumstances of the students they teach.

Schools can avoid much controversy by requiring a divorced or separated parent to submit a court-certified copy of the custody section of the divorce decree to the school. This document will address custody and visitation arrangements and, sometimes, educational and tuition responsibilities.

Teachers and administrators should bear in mind that they cannot protect a child against every possible threat. Parents should be instructed to tell their children not to get in the car or go with a noncustodial parent. Most children are of an age that a court would presume mental competency to assume the risk of their behavior. Obviously, the standard of care will be higher for younger children than for older children and/or adolescents.

The Catholic school teacher should be sensitive to the needs of children whose parents are divorced or separated. At the same time, parents need to understand that the school and its officials cannot guarantee the absolute safety of any child. Although administrators should assure parents that school officials will do everything they can, it must be noted that both the custodial parent and the child must bear some responsibility.

13. *False. Teachers in Catholic schools cannot be required to attend religious services or to participate in any religious activity.*

Teachers *can* be required to attend religious services and/or activities. However, administrators should not require that teachers participate actively if they do not wish to do so. For example, a teacher can be expected to accompany a class to a service and remain with the class throughout the service; participation should not be coerced. Non-Catholic teachers should not be expected to kneel, to sing, and so forth unless they freely choose to do so. A Catholic school can rightfully expect both the Catholic teacher's presence and participation, although, of course, the reception of Communion cannot be mandated. There are times when a Catholic school teacher may not wish to attend a service because of some personal situation or difficulty; such situations can and should be handled on an individual basis by the principal.

It is advisable to anticipate potential problem areas before hiring persons of other faiths. Frank discussion before a teacher begins work in a Catholic school can prevent misunderstanding at a later date.

CHAPTER THREE

What Laws Affect Catholic Schools?

One very important source of law governing Catholic education is canon law, or the law of the Catholic Church, which governs the existence of Catholic schools and their relationships with various persons and institutions within the church. A thorough consideration of canon law is beyond the scope of this work. Nonetheless, it is necessary to understand that canon law does set parameters around Catholic education.

Catholic schools can begin and sustain life as Catholic institutions only with the approval of the bishop. Canon 803, § 3 states, "Even if it is in fact Catholic, no school is to bear the name Catholic school without the consent of competent ecclesiastical authority [bishop]." All Catholic schools and personnel are subject to the bishop in matters of faith and morals and in any other matters prescribed by canon law.

There appear to be four main types of Catholic schools in the United States today. One is the diocesan school model that is ultimately governed by the bishop. Diocesan Catholic high schools have a distinguished history in the church. These high schools are usually established by the bishop and are under his direct authority.

The parish school represents a second type. Grade schools have traditionally been associated with, and supported by, parishes, and the pastor has been the person who has the proverbial last word, subject to the authority of the bishop. In current conditions of consolidation and regionalization of parishes, consolidation and regionalization of schools present a variation of the parish school model. Different governance configurations may exist for these schools: some are governed by boards with pastors of all the schools given seats on the board; others are governed by boards subject to the authority of the pastor or other individual who may be designated as the "canonical vicar." Still other diocesan grade schools have been established without any parish affiliation; a board in such a school may be under the direct jurisdiction of the bishop.

A third type of school is one owned by a religious congregation. The school is usually subject to the authority of a provincial, regional, or general superior. School boards exist at the invitation of the authority in the religious community. These schools are, like all others, subject to the authority of the bishop in matters concerning faith and morals.

A fourth type of school exists that is governed and/or owned by a board of trustees. A religious congregation may have decided to withdraw financial support from the school. If the congregation owned the school property, the leadership may have sold the school to a lay board of trustees for a nominal sum, with a provision that if the property and buildings were no longer used as a school, the property would revert to the congregation. These schools, too, are subject to the authority of the bishop in faith and morals.

CIVIL LAW

There are four major sources of civil law affecting Catholic education today: constitutional law, both state and federal; statutes and regulations; common law; and contract law.

CONSTITUTIONAL LAW

Constitutional law is the main source of the law for public education. In the majority of public school student dismissal cases, students allege deprivation of a constitutional right such as due process, governed by the U. S. Constitution. Students and teachers can claim constitutional rights because the public school is a government agency and public school administrators are state agents. The Constitution protects persons from arbitrary governmental deprivation of their constitutional freedoms. Students and teachers in Catholic schools cannot claim such protections because Catholic schools are private institutions administered by private persons.

Therefore, what cannot be done lawfully in a public school may be done in a Catholic school: For example, Catholic schools can restrict rights to freedom of expression; such restrictions would not be permitted in a public school because they are violations of the First Amendment's protection of free speech.

The United States Constitution is silent on the subject of education. The Tenth Amendment to the Constitution gives states any powers that are not previously expressly reserved to the federal government. Thus state government and state legislatures control public education so long as no constitutional protections are infringed.

STATUTES AND REGULATIONS

Federal and state statutes and regulations govern the public school and may govern the private school as well. If a statute requires that *all* who operate an educational institution within a given state follow a certain directive, both private and public schools are bound.

Federal antidiscrimination statutes, for instance, can bind on Catholic schools. Most dioceses now file statements of compliance with federal antidiscrimination laws with appropriate local, state, and national authorities. Catholic schools cannot discriminate on the basis of race, sex, color, national origin, age, or disability if, with reasonable accommodation, the person can perform the requirements of the job. Sex can be used as a condition of employment and/or enrollment if the school has a tradition of being a single-sex school.

Special Education

Catholic school teachers often have great concerns about their ability to meet the requirements of students with special needs. Some Catholic schools have taken the position that no accommodations will be made. Such a position is hardly consistent with the gospel and may pose legal issues as well. Several laws can affect Catholic schools. Section 504 of the Rehabilitation Act of 1973 (amended 1974), Public Law 94-142, the Education of All Handicapped Children Act, and the Individuals with Disabilities in Education Act are often cited in litigation brought against private schools who refuse to accommodate special needs.

Catholic school principals and staffs need to consider seriously what they can do to accommodate at least some special needs. Obviously, some needs cannot be met; most Catholic schools do not have the financial base to support sign-language interpreters, for example. But other needs can be met. A student who needs to tape-record classes should be allowed to do so, even though teachers may find it inconvenient. Catholic school officials do have a right to set minimum acceptance standards, and schools that are not equipped for dealing with serious mental disabilities would not be required to expend exorbitant amounts of money for the necessary accommodations. Further, no private school can be required to make an accommodation if the making of the accommodation would bankrupt the school; financial exigency is always a reason for Catholic schools to decline acceptance to special needs students so long as the financial exigency is true.

All involved in Catholic education should consider the *Pastoral Statement of U.S. Catholic Bishops on Handicapped People* (1988) in which the bishops reaffirmed the right of disabled persons to the services of the Catholic Church. A Catholic education is one such service. There are many accommodations that can be made without significant expense. The hiring of special education consultants/teachers in Catholic schools is making accommodation of special needs more of a reality.

Religious Discrimination

Catholic schools can discriminate on the basis of religion. Catholic schools can admit or give preference only to Catholic students. Similarly, Catholic teachers can receive preference in hiring because religion can be considered a *bona fide occupational qualification*. The 1980 case *Dolter v. Wahlert* demonstrates this: Ms. Dolter, an unmarried teacher in a Catholic school, became pregnant. In spite of the teacher's pregnancy, the principal gave her a contract for the following year. He later rescinded the contract, and the teacher brought suit. The principal maintained that his action was protected by the First Amendment's free exercise of religion clause. He stated that the Catholic Church forbids premarital sex and that the teacher would not present an acceptable role model for her students. The teacher presented evidence indicating that men who were known to have engaged in premarital sex were retained on the faculty.

The court ruled that the issue in this case was not premarital sexual immorality but rather sexual discrimination. The court found that the teacher was dismissed because of her pregnancy, not because of the premarital sexual activity. In a somewhat humorous footnote in the case, the court states, "The court can certainly take judicial notice of the fact that under the present physiological rules of nature women are the only members of the human population who can become pregnant" (p. 270). Ms. Dolter won her case and was able to collect damages.

The reason that antidiscrimination legislation can impact Catholic schools is that the government has a compelling interest in the equal treatment of all citizens. Compliance with the statute will be required if there is no less burdensome way to meet the requirements of the law.

COMMON LAW

A third source of civil law is common law. Common law is that body of case law that has been handed down through the ages. *Black's Law Dictionary* defines *common law:*

> "Common law" consists of those principles, usage and rules of action applicable to the government and security of persons and property which do not rest for their authority upon the express and positive declaration of the will of the legislature (p. 251).

The U.S. system of law is based on English law. Lawyers and judges search for precedents not only in the cases decided in the United States, but also in cases decided in English law before the United States came into existence.

CONTRACT LAW

The fourth source of the law governing both public and private schools is contract law. A contract consists of the following elements: (1) mutual assent (2) by legally competent parties (3) for consideration (4) to subject matter that is legal and (5) is stated in a form prescribed by law.

Mutual assent implies that two persons freely give consent to an agreement. Within the contractual framework, each incurs a detriment and each receives a benefit from the contract. A teacher agrees to teach in a Catholic school, a type of detriment in terms of being unable to perform other full-time work, and the teacher receives a benefit, payment of a salary. The contracting school incurs a detriment in terms of payment of money for salary and a benefit in that the students are being taught by a competent person.

The parties to a contract must be *legally competent.* The principal of the school or other contracting agent must possess the necessary authority to enter into a contract and bind the school. The parents possess the proper authority to enroll children in the school and to agree to pay tuition. The teacher must possess the minimum requirements for teaching and must not misrepresent personal qualifications.

In the case of *Bischoff v. Brothers of the Sacred Heart,* a laicized priest applied for the position of head of the religion department. He neglected to mention that he had been divorced and remarried without an annulment of the first marriage. When school administrators learned of these facts, the man's contract was rescinded, and he sued for breach of contract. The court ruled that the man was not legally competent to enter into a contract to be head of the religion department in a Catholic school because he could not be considered to be a Catholic "in good standing."

From a strictly legal standpoint, a Catholic school enters into a contract with parents, not students. Persons under the age of 18 are generally not legally competent to enter into a contract. Schools may require that students sign contracts agreeing to be bound by the rules of the school, but it is the signature(s) of the parent(s) that is (are) necessary for enforcement.

Consideration is what one party agrees to do for another party in exchange for some service from the other party. It is the "detriment" and "benefit" embodied in the *mutual assent.*

Subject matter that is legal requires that contractual provisions be within the parameters of the law. For example, a Catholic school could not require that teachers refrain from dating persons of another race because such a condition would be considered a violation of antidiscrimination legislation.

Form prescribed by law simply requires that the agreement be stated in a form consistent with state law. Oral contracts are considered legal in the majority of states. However, written contracts offer much more protection to both parties than do oral ones, and the possibilities for misinterpretation are lessened.

Catholic school students and teachers who sue Catholic schools and their officials often allege violation of constitutional freedoms as well as breach of contract. To date, no court has found that students and/or teachers in Catholic schools have any constitutional protections within the confines of the Catholic school.

To require that a Catholic school grant constitutional freedoms to students and teachers, a court must find that *state action* is present in the school. Two Catholic school student discipline cases are especially illustrative.

In *Bright v. Isenbarger,* students who were suspended from school for the rest of the school year alleged violation of due process protections. They maintained that state action was present in the school. *State action* has been defined as:

> In general, term used in connection with claims under due process clause and Civil Rights Act for which a private citizen is seeking damages or redress because of improper governmental intrusion into his life. In determining whether an action complained of constitutes "state action" within the purview of the Fourteenth Amendment, court must examine whether sufficiently close nexus exists between state and challenged action so that the action may fairly be treated as that of the state itself (Black, p. 1262).

In *Bright* the plaintiffs alleged that state action existed in these ways: The state regulated the educational standards of nonpublic as well as public schools; the state granted nonpublic schools tax-exempt status; and the school received some aid from both the federal and state governments. The court ruled in favor of the defendants and stated that it found no significant state action present. The court commented that, even if state action were found, the plaintiffs would have to establish a nexus between the state action present and the contested activity, the suspension of the students, before an action of a Catholic school could be fairly considered an action of the state for Constitutional due process purposes.

In another case, *Geraci v. St. Xavier High School*, an expelled student invoked the state action argument, even though he had actively recruited a young man from another Catholic school to come to St. Xavier and throw a pie in the face of an unpopular teacher during a final exam. The court had to determine if state action were present in St. Xavier actions to such a degree that the act of expulsion could be deemed an action of the government. The court found no state action and ruled that Catholic schools are not bound by the due process requirements of the U.S. Constitution.

The *Geraci* court did not give Catholic schools approval to act any way they choose; rather, the court talked about "fundamental fairness." Fundamental fairness is sometimes used as a synonym for constitutional due process. Applied to a nonpublic school, fundamental fairness is akin to, but not synonymous with, constitutional due process.

The 1982 Supreme Court case *Rendell-Baker v. Kohn* has rendered the state action argument moot. In this case, dismissed teachers sought to invoke the state action theory after they were dismissed from a private school for treatment of emotionally disturbed students. More than 90 percent of the school's operating funds came from the state through payment of tuition for students placed there through public school determination that such placement was necessary and unavailable in the public sector. Nonetheless, the Supreme Court found that the amount of funding, significant though it was, did not constitute state action; no nexus was demonstrated between the school's dismissal of teachers and the school's reception of government monies. The preceding discussion illustrates the unlikelihood of a student or a teacher prevailing in a dispute with a private school because of the difficulty of demonstrating significant state action that is sufficient to determine that the contested activity is state action. Thus, students and teachers seeking redress for alleged Catholic school treatment must rely on the provisions of contract law rather than the protections of the Constitution.

Duties of Principals

The duties of principals can generally be placed under two headings: (1) developing and implementing rules and policies and (2) supervising teachers. The principal should be the person who develops rules and policies, even if some other party, such as a school board or pastor, has the right of final approval. The principal or school president, if there is one, should be viewed as the chief executive officer of the school and the educational expert. Principal expertise should be utilized in the determination of policy. Although board members and pastors can certainly suggest topics and even details for policies, it seems to be a misuse of the board's and pastor's time if either or both are spending much time in an area that is properly the domain of the principal.

Supervision of teachers is the principal's second important duty. Supervision can be discussed from a variety of viewpoints. Supervision is a formative experience; evaluation is a summative one. Catholic school principals generally engage in both activities. In actual practice, it is often difficult to distinguish between the two. It is not unusual for a teacher to ask a principal, "Are you coming to evaluate me today?" when the visit is clearly labeled as supervisory.

Supervision is important in a legal context for two reasons. First, supervision is quality control: Is the consumer getting what has been paid for? Is the teacher doing an adequate job of teaching? Parallels are easily seen in the business world—a supervisor makes judgments about both the quality and quantity of an employee's output. The principal must ascertain that the teacher is teaching the appropriate concepts (quality control) at an appropriate pace (quantity control).

The second aspect of supervision is equally important. Supervision is job and legal protection for the teacher. If a group of irate parents or a pastor or anyone were to demand that the teacher's employment be terminated for inadequate performance, the teacher can offer very little in the way of a defense if the principal has never supervised the teacher's performance.

A second area of protection is found in the situation in which a teacher is sued for malpractice—either failing to teach what the student was supposed to learn or teaching concepts poorly. A teacher summoned to court because of a lawsuit will be grateful for the supervisory data a principal can provide.

Duties of Teachers

Teachers also have two general duties under the law: (1) implementation of rules and policies and (2) supervision of students' safety and learning. A teacher is required to implement the rules and policies of the school even if he or she does not personally agree with them. If a teacher cannot support a given policy or rule and reasonable attempts at effecting change have failed, the teacher's only course of action is to resign from the situation. In school, as in life, bottom lines exist. Resigning from a school in such circumstances does not necessarily mean that either the teacher or the school is in the wrong. Most employers understand that some persons simply cannot function effectively in certain situations.

Supervision of the safety and learning of students is a most serious responsibility. Supervision is both a mental and a physical act. It is not sufficient that teachers be physically present to students; they must be mentally present as well. Negligence cases emerging in the 1990s and into the new millennium are *not* claiming that students were left unattended and so injuries occurred, but rather that a teacher *was* physically present but *was not* paying attention to the students. Study halls and playgrounds can be particularly dangerous areas. Teachers can become so absorbed in their work or in conversation with other teachers that they have no real sense of what the students are doing. If an accident or injury should occur, a court could determine that the teacher failed in mental supervision.

It can be difficult to pay constant attention to students, but courts expect that teachers will act in reasonable ways. Spontaneous accidents or injuries can and do occur; it is unlikely that a court will expect a teacher to have prevented a spontaneous occurrence when evidence indicates that no one could have been expected to foresee and prevent the injury. Nonetheless, it is crucial that teachers give their full attention to their students.

Although there are specific laws governing Catholic education, teachers must understand that the law is a living entity that is in a constant state of flux. Teachers should commit to continuing professional development in the field of school law.

CHAPTER FOUR

Why Lawsuits Happen and How to Avoid Them

If a student or parent sues a teacher, it is very likely that the teacher will be accused of having committed a civil tort. *Black's Law Dictionary* defines a *tort* as: "[a] private wrong or injury, other than breach of contract, for which the court will provide a remedy in the form of an action for damages" (p. 1335). There are five particular torts that seem to appear more frequently than others.

Malpractice

The tort of malpractice is well known in medical and legal professions, but it can also arise in educational settings. *Black's Law Dictionary* defines *malpractice*:

> Professional misconduct or unreasonable lack of skills.... Failure of one rendering professional services to exercise that degree of skill and learning commonly applied under all the circumstances in the community by the average prudent reputable member of the profession with the result of injury, loss or damage to the recipient of those services or to those entitled to rely upon them.

It is any professional misconduct, unreasonable lack of skill or fidelity in professional or fiduciary duties, evil practice, or illegal or immoral conduct (p. 864).

Many teachers have heard "horror" stories about teachers who have been accused of malpractice. Generally, litigants allege malpractice because a student has failed to learn a given skill or skills. The prime example of educational malpractice is the failure to read. Students and/or parents allege that the teacher either did not teach the student reading or failed to take the ordinary measures a teacher would be expected to take to ensure that a student is not promoted to the next grade if that student has not mastered reading.

Although student failure to read is probably the most notable example of educational malpractice, there are others. Failure to learn any basic skill in the three Rs—reading, writing, and arithmetic—may provide the basis for a malpractice suit. It is certainly possible, however, that students in higher grades may allege malpractice if low marks or inability to practice necessary skills results in the denial of a place in another educational institution.

Today, public policy appears to have shifted. Social promotion is no longer considered an appropriate response to the failure to master skills. The restriction of social promotion may result in a decrease in malpractice suits.

The written records of supervisory visits by the principal or other administrative persons offer one of the best protections a teacher possesses against a malpractice suit. Teachers should keep copies of all such supervisory reports in case they should ever be needed.

Another protection against successful malpractice suits is found in teachers' plan books. Unless the school retains all plan books, teachers should retain them indefinitely so that they will be readily available when needed.

Corporal Punishment

A second tort is corporal punishment. The vast majority of Catholic schools in the United States do not permit corporal punishment; once common, the use of corporal punishment makes teachers and administrators vulnerable to the civil torts of assault and battery. Assault is an apprehension of physical danger; battery is the undesired or offensive touching of another.

A very controversial 1977 U.S. Supreme Court case, *Ingraham v. Wright,* involving two public school students who were severely paddled, brought the topic to the attention of the public. In *Ingraham* the Court held that there is no Eighth Amendment protection against cruel and unusual punishment for school children, private or public. The Court maintained that the eye of the public was enough protection to prevent abuse of corporal punishment. Almost immediately after this case was decided, states began to pass laws prohibiting its use and making teachers and administrators liable for civil torts of assault and battery.

Some case law promulgated after *Ingraham* should provide food for thought for all educators. Although the vast majority of corporal punishment lawsuits are brought in the public sector and involve constitutional due process issues, Catholic school teachers should be able to see the possibilities for similar arguments being made in Catholic schools because of the common law standards of fairness, good faith, and fair dealing. Catholic school personnel are not immune to civil tort cases if corporal punishment results in student injury.

Some readers may think, "We are not allowed to use corporal punishment anyway, so why talk about it?" Most educators do not realize the breadth of the definition of corporal punishment; it is not merely hitting a child with one's hand or with an object. Corporal punishment is any touching that can be construed as punitive. This writer once encountered a case in which an eighth grade teacher had lightly tapped a misbehaving student with a manila folder. The child's mother filed child abuse charges against the teacher. Of course, the teacher was exonerated, but the embarrassment and other negative effects lingered.

All educators should promise themselves the following: I will never touch a student in a way that could be construed as punitive. Therefore, Catholic school educators would be well advised to use other means of discipline than physical ones; such a stance is most appropriate from the standpoints of lawsuit avoidance and of fidelity to the philosophy and mission of Catholic schools.

Teachers should remember, though, that courts have consistently upheld the right of an educator to use physical force to restrain a student when anyone's safety is at stake. The court expects that a person will use self-defense if attacked. One does not waive the right of self-defense when one becomes a teacher. As always, the court will seek to determine if a teacher's actions fall within the "reasonable person" guideline: What would a reasonable person in the teacher's position have done?

Search and Seizure

A third tort arising in schools is search and seizure. The Fourth Amendment to the U.S. Constitution guarantees that

> [t]he right of the people to be secure in their persons, houses, papers and effects, against unreasonable searches and seizures, shall not be violated, and no Warrants shall issue, but upon probable cause, supported by oath or affirmation, and particularly describing the place to be searched, and the persons or things to be seized.

Although there are no cases involving search and seizure in Catholic schools that have reached the U.S. Supreme Court, in 1985 the Supreme Court decided the controversial public school case of *New Jersey v. T.L.O.* TLO was a high school student who had been accused of smoking. When the vice-principal confronted her, she denied the accusation. The vice-principal conducted a search of TLO's purse: It contained a quantity of marijuana, some rolling papers, a rather large amount of money, and an index card containing records of student drug transactions.

The vice-principal called the police who took the girl into custody. In a juvenile court proceeding, the student was placed on probation. She subsequently filed a suit against both the vice-principal and the school. TLO alleged that the vice-principal's search was impermissible under the provisions of the Fourth Amendment; she relied on the "fruit of the poisonous tree" doctrine which holds that if any part of the search is illegal, the fruit—whatever evidence is found—is poisoned.

In the light of cases such as *Tinker*, many school-law experts expected the student to prevail. In fact, she did not. The court held that although the public school is an agent of the state, public school officials would be held to a reasonable rather than a probable cause standard in search and seizure. Probable cause is a stricter standard than reasonable cause. The court listed examples of what might constitute reasonable cause; the list includes suspicious behaviors, such as anonymous notes and phone calls.

The rationale for holding public school administrators to a less strict standard than that to which other public officials are held in search and seizure situations is primarily based on the in loco parentis doctrine: School officials have the right to act as reasonable parents would if they suspected a child to be in possession of some illegal or dangerous substance. Also, like parents, school officials are supposed to provide for the safety of students and, therefore, looking for dangerous substances can be considered part of the duty of providing for that safety. Catholic school teachers and administrators are not held to the reasonable cause standard. However, Catholic schools should have some policy for searching students and/or seizing their possessions.

Searching a student's person or clothes should require more cause than searching a locker.

It should be noted that Catholic school teachers can be subject to tort suits if harm is alleged to have been done to a student because of an unreasonable search. Such harm does not have to be physical; psychological or emotional harm that would meet the common law requirements of torts may be sufficient. Additionally, Catholic school personnel, like their public school counterparts, could be charged with assault and battery and/or invasion of privacy if the search is found to be totally without merit.

A court will obviously examine more seriously alleged torts in search and seizure situations involving some kind of body search than it would a locker search. A teacher contemplating a search should weigh the value of what is being sought by the search against the harm that could result from the search. For example, if a small child says that she brought a dollar to school for lunch and the dollar is now missing, a full-scale search is probably not in order. After asking everyone to help to look for the dollar, the teacher could simply lend the child a dollar.

However, if an elementary school student were to inform the teacher that an expensive item of jewelry had been lost, the teacher would probably want to look for the item, for the sake of good parent/teacher relations, if nothing else. As always, approach is everything. A teacher could ask everyone to look in his or her pockets, desks, knapsacks, and so forth to see if the missing item could have gotten into someone's possession by mistake. The teacher can look in his or her own pockets and desk as well. This approach lessens the risk that a child will claim wrongful accusation. The teacher can deal privately with the student who has the missing item. Under no circumstances should a teacher threaten an entire class with being confined until the missing item returns. Aside from problems associated with making accusations against the whole class, the teacher is also punishing the entire group for something that only one person may have done. Also, some student claims allege that such conduct constitutes false imprisonment, although courts rarely give any serious consideration to such claims.

Defamation

Defamation is an unprivileged communication. One person reveals something about another person to a third person who is not privileged to receive it. *Black's Law Dictionary* provides the following definition:

> Defamation is that which tends to injure the reputation, to diminish the esteem, respect, goodwill or confidence in which the plaintiff is held, or to excite adverse, derogatory or unpleasant feelings or opinions against him.... A communication is defamatory if it tends to harm the reputation of another as to lower him in the estimation of the community or to deter third persons from associating or dealing with him (p. 375).

This definition describes a seemingly unreasonable action, one that is based on falsehood. Some people believe that the truth is an absolute defense; that is, if what a person says about another individual is true, that individual is precluded from recovering damages.

In the case of teachers, it is not uncommon for a judge and/or jury to invoke the "higher standard" to which teachers are sometimes held. This standard requires that teachers be judged by a stricter standard than that to which others are held because teachers hold a greater trust than the general public. Indeed, Jesus' words in the gospel indicate just such a standard: "To whom much is given, much will be required."

Defamation is a twin tort encompassing both slander and libel. Slander involves the spoken word, and it is generally harder to prove than libel, which involves the written word.

Teachers can almost unwittingly be drawn into slander. Certain places, such as faculty rooms, have long been considered safe havens in which faculty members can express feelings. So long as only the school's professional staff members are in the faculty room, the "safe haven" theory may apply, but if others, such as custodians, parents, volunteers, and/or visitors, are present, the faculty room is no longer a place for privileged communications, and a teacher risks being accused of slander if critical or derogatory comments are made about a student.

Social gatherings also present risks. If a parent approaches a teacher with a statement such as, "My daughter has been hanging around with Johnny B. I don't think much of him. What do you think?" and the teacher responds with a statement such as, "If I had a daughter, I wouldn't want her running around with him" or some similar derogatory statement, the teacher could well be found to have engaged in defamation of character, unprivileged derogatory communication. Teachers should always avoid even the appearance of defamatory speech and thus should avoid giving opinions concerning students to persons who have no particular right to know.

Libel is generally easier to prove than slander. If something does not need to be documented, it is better not to do so. Teachers should avoid making statements that are personal, rather than professional, opinions. "I feel that Johnny will not graduate from college" is a statement based on personal opinion. A better statement might be "In determining the admission of John to the engineering program at your university, you may wish to consider the following factors: class rank, grade point average, extracurricular involvement, and so forth." This statement directs the attention of the admissions committee to facts that are specific, behaviorally oriented, and verifiable. Those facts may well present the student in a less than favorable light, but the teacher has behaved in an appropriate, professional manner. Further, the admissions committee is a party with the right to be told these facts.

Questions often arise concerning situations in which teachers are asked to write recommendations for students. Obviously, if a teacher wants to write positive comments about a student, the likelihood that a student will object is minimal. The problem occurs when a teacher cannot, in conscience, write a favorable recommendation for a student. The teacher, then, can refuse to write a recommendation; after all, no one has an absolute legal right to a recommendation. There can be serious repercussions, however, if a school requires a certain subject matter or grade level teacher to answer questions. Teachers may well question the fairness of telling students that they, the teachers, cannot fill out certain forms if the forms are required for admission consideration. In such circumstances, the teacher may opt for a general letter of reference, which does little more than verify that the teacher did indeed teach the student. A teacher has every right to decline to complete a form and, instead, write and attach a letter to the form. Such a letter might read as follows:

To Whom It May Concern:

This letter will verify that John Jones was a student in my eighth grade class this year. I taught John language arts and social science. In language arts, we used such and such a text. We studied these concepts: (list concepts). John's average was _____. In social science (as above).

This kind of letter says nothing derogatory about John; one could argue that it says nothing substantive about John either. The individual receiving the letter should be able to tell that it is not an overwhelming affirmation of John's credentials for admission. But the letter contains nothing that a teacher could be criticized for writing. What is written is specific, behaviorally oriented, and verifiable. The teacher might conclude such a letter with an innocuous statement such as "I am sure John will make a unique contribution to your school," "You will not soon forget John," or similar phrases.

Teacher comments on student report cards and/or permanent record cards pose another concern. If student report cards are simply reporting mechanisms to parents and the permanent record card is the actual retained record, teachers have considerable leeway in making comments. Parents have a "right to know," and although a parent might dispute the accuracy of a teacher's comment, it would be difficult to demonstrate any actual harm to student reputation. If, however, persons without any need or right to know view permanent record cards and/or transcripts, legal problems can result.

The days of individuals' being denied access to their records ended with the Buckley Amendment, which guarantees parents and students access to records. School administrators should ensure that no personal and/or subjective comments are written on documents contained in student files. Materials that are subjective in nature can and should be stored elsewhere. Disciplinary records, in particular, should be housed in files separate from those containing permanent records. In summary, then, a teacher's best protection is to write only what is necessary and to write in objective terms.

Negligence

A large number of cases brought against teachers allege negligence. *Negligence* has been defined as a failure to exercise the degree of care owed to an individual, which results in injury to the individual. Four elements must be present before a court can render a finding of negligence. If one of these elements is missing, negligence is not present. These elements are: (1) duty, (2) violation of duty, (3) proximate cause, and (4) injury.

A teacher must possess a *duty* in a given situation. If a teacher is attending a professional football game and encounters two students fighting, the teacher has no duty to intervene. Even if the students suffer injuries, the teacher cannot be legally negligent because teachers have no legal duty to minors at football games, unless it is a school football game. If a teacher in such a situation were to be accused of negligence, the teacher would have to be exonerated because one cannot be negligent toward another if one has no duty to the other.

A classic example often given in tort consideration involves an individual who is driving on a dark road late at night, sees a wrecked car, gets out to investigate, and discovers an injured person in the wrecked car. The first individual has no legal duty to render assistance to the injured person. The driver can return to the car and drive away without giving any aid. Although one could easily maintain that a moral or ethical duty had been violated, one cannot maintain that a legal duty has been violated. Some educators may decry the actions of a teacher who makes no attempt to stop a fight between students in a public place as inappropriate, but the teacher will not be found liable for legal negligence. Of course, failure to intervene in a fight at recess when the teacher is presiding could produce very different results.

Students have a right to safety, and teachers have a responsibility to protect all students in their care. Reasonable people can assume that teachers have a duty to supervise student behavior so that injuries do not occur. At first glance, such statements seem self-evident. However, there are gray areas in which it is not so easy to determine whether teachers have duties.

Is the teacher responsible for supervising the behavior of students who arrive at school early? If the teacher allows the students to congregate in her classroom, is she responsible if student injury occurs? Would she be better advised to refuse students admission to her classroom when they arrive before school is officially open?

These are difficult questions and there are no simple answers. Case law, dating from more than thirty years ago, indicates that schools and their officials can be held responsible for accidents occurring on school property if they knew or should have known of the danger. In the 1967 case of *Titus v. Lindberg*, a school administrator was found liable for student injury occurring on school grounds before the official opening time because: he knew that students arrived at school before the official opening time; he was present on the campus when they were; he had established no rules for student conduct outside the building, nor had he provided for the supervision of the students. The court found that he did have a duty to supervise.

Courts generally return to that fictional entity, the reasonable person, to determine the degree, if any, of liability. In the *Titus* case, the court ruled that a reasonable person in the principal's position would have provided some supervision. It is less clear how a teacher would have fared if the injury had occurred in a classroom before the official opening time but when a teacher was present. A court could decide that once a teacher allows students to enter the classroom before the official opening time, the teacher has assumed a supervisory duty that might not otherwise have been present. The importance of clear policies and procedures as well as the delineation of responsibilities is evident. Teachers who find themselves in the unenviable position of supervising students before the official opening time simply because they are in their classrooms should encourage the principal to discuss the situation with all appropriate parties and work toward a reasonable policy for early arrivals and after school lingerers.

The second element is *violation of duty*. There can be no negligence if no violation of duty occurred. For example, if a teacher is supervising students on a playground and a child spontaneously picks up a rock, throws it, and injures another child, the teacher should not be held liable. The teacher had no way of knowing and/or preventing the spontaneous action of the child. Liability might result if it could be demonstrated that this particular child had engaged in rock throwing on other occasions and the teacher took no steps to correct the situation, or if a teacher, through laziness or inattention, allowed rock throwing to continue.

The third element of negligence is *proximate cause*, which is distinguished from direct cause. If a child hits another with a rock, the child's throwing of the rock is the direct cause of the student injury.

The supervising teacher may be the proximate cause if his action or inaction contributed to the injury. *Proximate cause* has also been defined as a "contributing factor"; in other words, would the child have been injured if the teacher had properly supervised? Proximate cause is a "but for" condition; if the teacher had done or not done the thing that he did, the child would not have been injured.

The tragedy that occurred in the *Levandowski v. Jackson City School District* case demonstrates the concept of proximate cause. A teacher failed to report a thirteen-year-old girl as missing from her class when the girl failed to report to class, and her name was not on the absentee list. The child's body was later found floating in a river. The mother filed suit and alleged that, if her daughter's absence had been properly reported, her death could have been averted. The court, however, ruled for the teacher and the school because the mother failed to demonstrate a causal link between the teacher's violation of duty and the death of the child. The *Levandowski* case is an example of a failure in proximate cause. The reader should note that the teacher did have a duty, the teacher did violate the duty, and there was an injury. The circumstances of this case indicated that no causal link existed between the teacher's violation of duty and the injury. Changing the facts a bit could create a much different scenario. Suppose, for example, that the student had been found murdered in a school bathroom or under the front steps of the school. In such circumstances, the mother might well have prevailed, as the causal link between the violation of duty and the injury would be easier to demonstrate.

Another often-cited example of proximate cause is provided by the case of *Smith v. Archbishop of St. Louis*. A second grade teacher kept a lighted candle on her desk every morning in May to honor the Mother of God. She gave no special instructions regarding candles and/or fire. On the day of a school play, the Smith child was assigned to play the part of a bird. Her costume was composed partially of crepe paper, and when she walked too close to the candle, her costume caught fire. The teacher tried to extinguish the fire and was severely burned in the process. The child sustained serious psychological problems as well as severe facial and upper body burns that required ongoing painful treatments. The archdiocese maintained that the incident was the result of an accident. The court ruled that, while the mishap was an accident, it was a *foreseeable* accident. Referring to the case of *Ziegler v. Santa Cruz High School District*, the court discussed forseeability:

> Negligent supervision, like any other tort, involves a breach of a duty defendant owes plaintiff which causes plaintiff to suffer damage.... To recover, plaintiff need not show that the very injury resulting from defendant's negligence was foreseeable, but merely that a reasonable person could have foreseen that injuries of the type suffered would be likely to occur under the circumstances (p. 251).

The *Smith* case provides teachers with much food for thought. It underscores the importance of teachers taking time periodically to consider their specific circumstances in light of the potential for danger and to take appropriate steps to eliminate or at least minimize the possibilities for harm.

The fourth element necessary for a finding of negligence is injury. Educators often equate negligence and irresponsible behavior, but the two terms can be distinguished. No matter how irresponsible a teacher's behavior is, the teacher is innocent of "legal" negligence if the irresponsibility did not contribute to the injury.

The classroom is the place where most accidents occur. Students and teachers spend most of their time in classrooms; therefore, it is logical that most accidents occur there. Other areas are more dangerous than classrooms, and teachers must exercise extreme caution when supervising students in these places. Shop and lab classes contain greater potential for injury, and case law indicates that courts expect teachers to exercise a greater degree of care than they would in ordinary classrooms. Teachers and administrators are further expected to ensure that equipment is in working order and that areas are free of unnecessary hazards. Teachers are expected to give students safety instructions concerning hazards and the use of dangerous equipment.

Athletics pose special problems because the chances for student injury during athletics are high. Principals should ensure that: coaches are properly trained and possess the necessary competencies; clear procedures are followed in accidents and emergencies; equipment is in working order; and playing areas are as hazard-free as possible.

A teacher who is asked to serve as a coach should not accept the position unless the conditions set forth in the preceding paragraph are met. Teachers who are coaches should be certified in standard first aid and should know how to give CPR; athletic directors and other administrators should require that another competent adult be present or nearby when practices and games are held so that medical and other help can be obtained if needed, as well as to provide supervision for the group if one student has to be taken to a hospital.

Negligence is the most often litigated tort. Some other examples of tort situations that could result in liability follow.

Child Abuse/Neglect/Sexual Abuse Reporting

All fifty states have laws requiring educators to report suspected child abuse, neglect, and/or sexual abuse. Although the actual wording may vary somewhat from state to state, the law may contain words such as, "Any teacher, principal, nurse, counselor, doctor, and so forth who knows or has reason to believe that a child is being abused or neglected must report the suspicion to the police or other appropriate authority."

Law enforcement officials and attorneys tell teachers to report anything that a child tells them in the area of neglect and/or abuse. They will further caution teachers that it is not a teacher's job to determine if abuse has occurred; the teacher's function is to present the information.

The appropriate people will make the determination as to whether agency involvement is appropriate.

School administrators should ensure that teachers are provided with in-service training concerning the indicators of child abuse and neglect, as well as the legal procedures for reporting abuse and neglect. There are many excellent written resources available for education in this area. Local police departments and social service agencies can provide both materials and speakers. If a school does not provide teachers with education and materials on the topic, a phone call to appropriate sources should provide the teacher with needed information.

States generally have statutes mandating that a person cannot be held liable for making a good faith report of child abuse or neglect. However, a person can be held liable for making what is referred to as a malicious report. A malicious report is one that has no basis in fact and was made by a person who knew that no factual basis existed. Conversely, statutes usually mandate that a person who knew of child abuse or neglect and failed to report it can be fined and/or charged with a misdemeanor or felony.

Nothing that is stated above is intended to suggest that reporting child abuse and neglect is easy. Difficult and/or doubtful cases require "judgment calls." A teacher would be well advised to discuss suspicions with another teacher and/or the principal. Teachers must bear in mind, however, that they have the ultimate responsibility to make the report to the proper authorities. Whenever a teacher makes a report, the principal should be informed.

Records and Confidentiality

As stated earlier, teachers must guard against writing anything in a student record that cannot be verified, that is not stated in behavioral terms, and/or that is based on subjective opinion rather than objective fact.

Since the passage of the Buckley Amendment, the majority of Catholic schools have voluntarily complied with it. Parents and older students are routinely allowed access to student files. Teachers and administrators should ensure that nothing potentially defamatory is allowed to remain in a student's file without good reason for its inclusion.

The law relating to personnel records is less clear, particularly in the private sector. Personnel files should contain: (a) transcripts of academic work; (b) recommendations for employment; (c) records of observations and evaluations; (d) any teacher self-evaluations; and (e) disciplinary warnings or records. If there is no reason to have an item in a file, then it should not be placed there. For example, an administrator's personal notes regarding a conference or observation do not belong in a teacher's file, and their presence could prove problematic for both teacher and administrator. No unauthorized person, including members of the school board, should seek or be given access to student or personnel records. Fairness would require, it seems, that teachers in Catholic schools be: (1) allowed access to their personnel files; (2) given copies of all supervisory and evaluative forms and be allowed to add any desired comments to those forms. Nothing is gained and much can be lost if principals deny teachers access to their own records.

This chapter has discussed tort liability in light of existing laws. The next chapter will discuss faculty handbooks as contractual obligations.

CHAPTER FIVE

The Faculty Handbook:
Part of Your Contract

Catholic school teachers generally sign employment contracts each year. These contracts can be single-sheet forms or multipage documents in which the basic rights and responsibilities of each party to the contract are delineated. Unless explicitly excluded by the employment contract, faculty handbooks can be considered part of the contract, and the provisions of the handbooks can bind teachers. A teacher applying for a position in a Catholic school should carefully read both the employment contract and the faculty handbook before accepting a teaching position. This chapter will discuss the main topics usually found in faculty handbooks. Teachers often are, and should be, included in the discussion regarding construction, development, and/or revision of handbooks. A discussion of essential handbook elements should prove useful in the handbook development and implementation.

School Philosophy

The beginning point for any handbook development in a Catholic school should be the philosophy of the school. A philosophy answers the question, "What do we as Catholic educators say that we are doing in this school?" Persons accepting positions in a Catholic school should be familiar with the philosophy of the school and should be willing to commit themselves to making that philosophy a living reality in the school. Occasionally, one may find it impossible to accept the school's philosophy and, therefore, must decline employment.

All faculty members should "own" the school's philosophy. The administrator should provide opportunities for periodic review of the philosophy by all members of the school community. Each individual faculty member should reflect on the meaning of the philosophy at regular intervals. Aside from any educational or ministerial reasons for review, there are sound legal reasons. Courts have looked to philosophies in deciding difficult cases, and it behooves teachers to have an understanding of the requirements of the philosophy and their own lived experience of it.

Teaching Duties

The first category of duties that faculty handbooks address generally concerns teaching duties. It may appear that this category is a statement of the obvious. Although it is true that this category is usually not controversial because teachers expect to have teaching duties, the particular provisions of the category may generate some problems in interpretation and implementation. Teaching duties may be divided into four subsections: instruction of students; supervision of students; record keeping and grading; and professionalism/loyalty.

The faculty handbook should tell teachers *what* they are expected to do. The handbook need not tell teachers *how* to teach, but broad parameters should be offered. Teachers may be told what types of teaching techniques are recommended and what types should be avoided.

Persons to be consulted for help (principal, assistant principal, department heads, level coordinators, etc.), should be listed.

Approximate length and time requirements of homework assignments should be indicated. Teachers should not hesitate to seek help when needed. Should a teacher be faced with dismissal and assert that no help was ever given to remedy problems, it will be difficult for the assertion to be of much use if the faculty handbook clearly listed sources of help and the teacher failed to make use of them.

A second subsection is supervision of students within the classroom setting. The fact that supervision is a mental as well as a physical act should be emphasized. Procedures for dealing with situations in which a teacher must leave a class unattended should be addressed. At minimum, the teacher should have a plan for student behavior when the teacher is absent; this plan should be discussed with students on a regular basis and/or posted prominently as part of classroom rules.

The faculty handbook should provide guidance in a third area of teaching duties, record keeping and grading. The system of grading (letter, numeral, numeral equivalents, pass/fail) should be stated; teachers should study the system and should not deviate from it without the permission of the principal. If one teacher gives anyone with a grade of more than 90 an *A* and another teacher's *A* is based on grades of more than 93, problems are almost certain to occur.

Record keeping can also pose problems. School officials should require teachers to submit attendance records to the office where they should be kept indefinitely. It is not unusual for the police or the courts to ask teachers and/or other school officials to verify a student's attendance on a given day, sometimes many years after the student has left school. If teachers are given no directions in the handbook or from the principal, teachers should maintain attendance records in their own files.

Similarly, grade books and plan books should be kept on file. If the school does not maintain these records, the teacher should retain them in the event that a malpractice suit is brought against the teacher. These records may never be needed, but they are invaluable when litigation occurs.

A fourth subheading deals with professionalism and loyalty. Teachers are professionals and should conduct themselves accordingly. The employing institution has a right to expect that its employees will be loyal to the Catholic Church and to the institution.

Nonteaching Duties

A second broad area of handbook concern is nonteaching duties, which are often more problematic than teaching duties. It is in everyone's best interests that nonteaching duties be clearly outlined. Generally, a teacher can expect to have at least the following items discussed: cafeteria, playground, and study hall supervision; discipline; and extracurricular activities. Teachers should find handbook guidelines for supervising these areas. Teachers must understand that these duties require the same professional attention that classroom duties demand.

The student discipline code should be included in its entirety. School rules, penalties, exceptions, and appeals processes should be outlined. A Christian due process model should require that a student at least be given *notice* (this is, what you did that was wrong) and a *hearing* (a chance to present one's side) before an *impartial tribunal*, the teacher, imposes punishment.

Field trips are another area of nonteaching duties, although field trips should be an extension of the academic experience. Earlier in this text, the importance of proper permission forms was discussed. The faculty handbook should outline in detail the policies and procedures that are to be followed in taking students on field trips.

Field trip policies and procedures should answer such questions as: How is a trip initiated? Who approves the trip? How much advance notice is needed? How is the educational purpose of the trip indicated? What permission slip is to be used? How many chaperones are needed? What will students be assigned to do in lieu of the trip if the parent(s) do not wish the student to participate in the trip? Can students be excluded from the trip because of behavior and/or academic problems? What provisions, if any, will be made for students who forget to bring the signed form? How will the teacher check for forgery? What are the conduct rules for the trip? What are the penalties for violating the rules?

After reading the above list, a teacher may be tempted to think that a field trip is not worth the trouble, but most teachers believe that field trips are valuable extensions of the academic experience. Procuring answers to the above questions will help provide as safe and satisfying an experience as possible.

The use of a standard permission slip in both the school and diocese is invaluable. Permission slips should begin with a statement such as, "I request that the school allow my child to participate in the following activity." Clauses limiting the liability of the school should follow, such as:

> I hereby give permission for my child to participate in the activity. In consideration for the making of the arrangements for this experience, I (we) hereby release, indemnify, and hold harmless the school and any and all employees from any and all liability for any injury occurring while my child participates in the trip.

In addition, the educational purpose should be clearly stated.

Extracurricular activities are routinely part of the nonteaching duties of teachers. Teachers should be told how many, if any, extracurricular activities they can be assigned to moderate and what, if any, compensation will be offered. A moderator's checklist for activities should be included. Extracurricular activities used to be almost the exclusive domain of the high school. Today elementary schools may have as many extracurricular programs as the secondary schools. Athletics, yearbooks, drama, music productions, and other activities are all finding homes in elementary schools. Teachers have a right to know what their extracurricular activities will be prior to signing contracts and to be given as much direction in moderating these activities as possible.

A final area of nonteaching duties lies in attendance at meetings and other school events. Schools should have a policy governing faculty attendance at such times. Principals may find that issuing a yearly calendar is in the best interests of all so that people know early in the year which dates have claims on their time. A wise principal will reserve the right to require attendance at other meetings but will try to give teachers as much notice as possible for these unscheduled requirements.

Supervision and Evaluation of Teachers

A third contractual concern lies in the area of supervision and evaluation of teachers. The faculty handbook should state the school's policy on supervisory visits and on the evaluation process and should provide answers for the following questions: How often is a teacher observed? By whom? What is the format? Are pre- and post-conferences held? Does the principal reserve the right to make unscheduled visits? How are supervisory data utilized in evaluation? Are there components other than supervisory data that are part of evaluation? How may teachers express disagreement with supervisory and/or evaluative assignments? If questions such as these are not addressed in the faculty handbook, teachers owe it to themselves to request answers.

Teachers should always receive copies of supervisory instruments; if copies are not offered, teachers should respectfully request them. Teachers should always sign supervisory instruments so that there can be no doubt that they saw and discussed the contents of the instruments. A signature does not indicate teacher agreement; rather, it merely demonstrates that the teacher has received and read the document. In the interest of fairness, teachers should be allowed to append any written comments they desire; in effect, they should be allowed to disagree with the data contained in the supervisory or evaluative instrument. Aside from being good legal practice, such procedures model fairness to the school community.

It is not advisable to keep supervisory, evaluative, and/or disciplinary records secret. In the event of any litigation surrounding termination or nonrenewal of contract, a judge will examine the behavior of both parties to see if those behaviors are fair and reasonable. Denying teachers access to documents pertaining to their employment is simply not fair. Sharing supervisory and evaluative instruments promotes an atmosphere of healthy communication.

Important Policies to Consider

Most faculty handbooks contain the personnel policies of the school. Some handbooks do not discuss items such as sick leave, personal leave, maternity leave, bereavement leave, and other types of leave. Pastors and principals attempt to handle such situations on a case-by-case basis. Many problems can ensue. Some hardworking teachers will not take time off, even with legitimate need, because their colleagues would have to add to their duties in an effort to "cover" the absent teacher's classes. Conversely, some individuals abuse the process because there is no upper limit on leave taking. The practice of deciding to grant leave on an individual basis is fraught with difficulty and leaves principals open to charges of favoritism.

Clear policies can help everyone. Principals can and should reserve the right to make exceptions to policies for extraordinary reasons; teachers should be able to present special circumstances to a principal.

The practice of allowing sick days to accumulate helps persons to take time off when needed but guards against misuse. If there is no allowance for accumulation, some teachers may be tempted to take ten or more sick days a year.

Catholic schools need to have grievance policies in place. It is easier to develop a policy that is never needed than to construct one when needed. Disagreements between faculty and administrators do occur, and people have a right to a forum in which to discuss such disagreements. Such a procedure is certainly consistent with the gospel mandate, "If you are bringing your gift to the altar and remember that you are angry with your brother [or sister], leave your gift at the altar and go and make peace with your brother [or sister]. Then, return to the altar and offer your gift." A clear grievance procedure offers both teachers and administrators good legal protection and models gospel values. If steps in a grievance procedure are followed, both sides possess evidence of dealing in good faith.

Teacher job protection policies, if any, should be found in the faculty handbook. Some might argue that there is no real job protection in a Catholic school, and, to some extent, that is correct. The U.S. Supreme Court, which determines the supreme law of the land, has yet to hear a Catholic school termination case.

The concept of tenure is one that has been largely avoided by Catholic elementary and secondary schools, except those who had unions in place prior to the 1979 decision, *NLRB v. Catholic Bishop of Chicago*, which held that Catholic schools did not have to permit unions. Tenure is defined as an expectation of continuing employment. In the public school, tenure is a substantive property right protected by the Fifth and Fourteenth Amendments to the Constitution. There have been some indications that courts will examine the fair-play element involved in nontenured teacher dismissals.

Catholic school administrators would be well advised to have policies and procedures in place when considering the dismissal of a teacher who has taught in the school for a length of time that would have resulted in tenure if the person had been in a public school. The concept of de facto tenure, tenure in fact, is often discussed; however, the concept has been ignored by recent court decisions and appears to be, for all practical purposes, an ineffective argument at this time.

Surely, however, the gospel and basic fairness demand that teachers and administrators in Catholic schools be given some type of job security after they have spent a certain number of years in ministry at a school.

The faculty handbook, then, is an important contractual obligation. In the same way, parents assume contractual obligations to the school when they enroll their children, and the parent/student handbook states those obligations. If a school does not have a parent/student handbook, teachers may wish to encourage and help the administrator in developing one. No one wants to become a slave to documents, but the more one can commit to writing, the less chance there is for misunderstanding and injustice.

CHAPTER SIX

Selected Issues

By the time the reader reaches Chapter Six, it should be apparent that the topic of civil law and Catholic schools is a broad area for consideration. The first five chapters of this text have dealt with general principles and some specific applications of those principles. This chapter will discuss four topics of special concern for educators in the new millennium. A few short years ago, these topics would have received scant, if any, mention in a discussion of school law. The topics are:

- staff/student relationships;
- personal conduct of professional staff;
- gangs; and
- school safety policies and violence prevention.

Staff/Student Relationships

The vast majority of Catholic school teachers are caring individuals who consider teaching as a ministry that extends to all areas of student life. Students routinely ask teachers for advice; it is not unusual for teachers to find themselves in the position of surrogate parents. Students often entrust adults with confidential information. Teachers may respond to a student's apparent need without considering the way others might interpret that response. Teaching careers can be ruined if someone alleges inappropriateness. Teachers must, therefore, avoid both the perception and the reality of inappropriateness. Few guidelines are available. Teachers often deal with situations that pose personal and legal risks for the adults as well as for the students. A relatively new type of lawsuit in which parents threaten and/or pursue legal action against a teacher whose actions they viewed as unwise, inappropriate, sexually motivated, or interfering with the parent/child relationship is emerging.

SEXUAL MISCONDUCT

Teachers can find themselves accused of sexual misconduct in apparently innocent situations. Students *can* misinterpret touching, and teachers face child abuse charges. Extreme caution is in order whenever an adult touches a student. A good test of one's behavior would be to ask, "What would I think if I saw someone else doing what I am about to do?"

A student who believes that a teacher has not responded to efforts to achieve a closer relationship presents another problematic situation. Such a student may accuse a teacher of inappropriate conduct as a retaliatory measure. Serious consequences can result from an allegation of child abuse, even if that allegation is eventually proven to be false. If a child abuse report is made, authorities will question the teacher and the investigation will be recorded. In some states, lists of suspected child abusers are kept.

State statutes require that teachers know the child abuse laws of the state and that they follow those statutes in their interactions with students.

Sexual harassment is a form of sexual misconduct. At the very simplest level, sexual harassment involves some kind of overt and implied sexual behavior directed toward a person who has neither invited nor accepted the behavior. Some specific examples of behaviors that could be considered sexual harassment are sexual propositions, off-color jokes, inappropriate physical contact, innuendoes, and sexual offers, looks, and gestures.

To avoid even the slightest hint of impropriety, a teacher should not tolerate any student sexual harassment of another. Teachers also should avoid being alone with a single student behind closed doors unless a window or other opening permits outsiders to see into the area. Fear of teachers facing child abuse allegations has caused some public school districts in this country to adopt rules that prohibit any faculty touching of students. No teacher would want to take such a position, but commonsense precautions must be taken for the protection of all.

EMOTIONAL INVOLVEMENT

Teachers must understand that they are professionals rendering a service. Just as a counselor or psychiatrist is professionally bound to avoid emotional involvement with a client, a teacher should avoid becoming so emotionally involved with a young person that objectivity and fairness are compromised. Teachers have many students for whom they are responsible and who need attention. If a relationship with a student keeps a teacher from responding to other student needs on a regular basis, the teacher and the principal or other supervisor should seriously examine the appropriateness of the relationship. In seeking to assess the appropriateness of an adult/student relationship, some mental health professionals recommend asking oneself questions such as these: Whose needs are being met? Is there a boundary? Where is it?

The following adult behaviors could be considered inappropriate, depending on the totality of the circumstances: dropping by a student's home, particularly if no parent is present; excessive letter writing; statements such as, "I love you"; frequent telephoning of the student; social trips with a student; and sharing of teacher's personal problems. The topic of student/teacher relationships merits careful reflection by teachers. Common sense, knowledge of the law, and a sense of prayer can help ensure that appropriate boundaries are set and maintained while meeting students' legitimate needs.

Personal Conduct of Professional Staff

The vast majority of Catholic school teachers probably realizes that they are considered role models. However, some teachers believe that they should be responsible to school and church officials only for conduct that occurs within the school day or the school setting. Yet, conduct outside the school setting as well as conduct inside the school setting can reflect negatively on the teacher, the school, and the parish.

BEHAVIORAL EXPECTATIONS FOR TEACHERS

Documents governing teacher employment should state that teachers are expected to behave in accordance with the teachings of the Catholic Church. Both Catholics and non-Catholics seeking teaching positions in Catholic settings should expect that standards of behavior would be in force. For example, if the fact that an individual had an abortion becomes known and is a source of scandal, the school has every right to terminate that individual's employment or volunteer status. To do otherwise might send a confusing message to parents, students, and the larger community.

ISSUES OF SEXUAL PREFERENCE AND/OR LIFESTYLE

Issues of sexual preference pose special problems. While no one should condemn a homosexual orientation, a Catholic school administrator as an agent of the church cannot ignore manifestations of an overt gay lifestyle that pose scandal.

Equally difficult decisions must be made in situations involving divorced staff members who remarry without an annulment if that fact becomes known. There is no easy solution, but teachers must understand that administrators have an obligation to see that the teachings of the Catholic Church are respected and not compromised. In summary, then, once an individual performs an act that is inconsistent with church teaching and that act becomes public knowledge, that person may no longer be qualified to teach in a Catholic school.

ILLEGAL ACTIVITY

A person who has committed an illegal act may certainly have employment terminated. One who is convicted of a crime or who admits commission of a crime should be removed from a teaching position. The harder question arises when a person is simply accused of a crime or is arrested on suspicion of a crime. The United States has long operated under the principle of "innocent until proven guilty." It may appear that until guilt is established, the fair approach would be to let the person continue in ministry. Yet, the reality often is that effectiveness in such situations is severely compromised. Virtually every diocese has some policy dealing with serious accusations of wrongdoing, and administrators should follow the diocesan directive(s). If no diocesan policy is in place, administrators and boards should develop individual school policies and procedures in this regard. As has been said earlier, it is better to have a policy you never need than to try to construct a policy to fit a particular situation.

Gangs

Today, the word *gang* has a much different meaning than it had twenty, thirty, or fifty years ago. Many readers remember their parents or grandparents referring to the good times they had while they "ran around with a gang of friends." Today, the word *gang* connotes fear, violence, and domination. Teachers may well be forced to deal with gangs and their effects.

The first step in developing policy is to define exactly what a gang is. Several courts have stated that the proper term to use when discussing problematic gangs is *criminal ganglike behavior.* Thus, both teacher and student should understand that the intent to commit criminal acts is what distinguishes criminal ganglike activity from other types of group activities. Moreover, it is not membership in a gang in and of itself that is the problem; it is the criminal activity.

Gang Attire, Symbols, and Behaviors

The wearing of colors has long indicated membership in a gang. School officials are well within their rights to forbid such displays. However, it is not always easy to identify what exactly is the display of gang colors. In one state, for example, two university athletic teams have different school colors. So gang members wear university sweatshirts, jackets, and so on to denote their membership in a particular gang. Certainly, there is nothing wrong with wearing a college sweatshirt, and it is very difficult, if not impossible, to determine who is supporting a team and who is displaying gang colors. Catholic teachers should enforce uniform regulations and/or dress codes and be attentive to violations of the codes.

DISCIPLINARY STEPS

If a teacher suspects or notices criminal ganglike activity at any time, the principal should be notified immediately. Second, the principal should seek appropriate advice concerning investigation of the suspicion or allegation and then proceed to gather necessary data. Third, if the principal determines or strongly suspects that the young person is involved in criminal ganglike activity, parents or guardians should be notified and disciplinary action taken when appropriate. In the case of suspicion without any convincing evidence, a warning concerning the consequences for any one who engages in criminal ganglike activity may be given. Written documentation of any meetings should be kept. If a criminal act has occurred, the administrator has a legal responsibility to notify local law enforcement officials and to assist the officials as far as possible in their investigation(s).

A teacher should focus on what was actually done that is/was wrong, rather than on membership in a gang. If a school rule has been broken, the breaking of the rule should be discussed and appropriate sanctions given. If a crime has been committed, the focus should be on the crime and its consequences.

Some young people recognize the dangers of criminal gang membership only after they have become members, and they may need help to terminate membership in a gang. Others may seek help in avoiding involvement with gangs. Teachers should have some training or know where to contact trained persons so that students can be helped to avoid gangs. Gone are the days when a principal or teacher could announce that some activity or association is wrong and expect immediate student compliance. It is every teacher's responsibility to help in the creation of a community in which persons have no desire to engage in criminal activity.

School Safety Policies and Violence Prevention

The topic of school safety and violence has been discussed earlier in the text. Teachers have serious responsibilities for the safety of students and others. No teacher can afford to be unconcerned about any possible risk to safety.

Recent school shootings strike fear in the heart of all responsible for children, teachers, and other members of the school community. The presence of criminal gangs and their attraction to youth may cause other young people to behave in ways that a few decades ago would not have been imagined. Policies and procedures must be in place to deal with the unthinkable. No one can adopt an attitude of "it will never happen here." Besides the tragedies that could occur, schools and employees could face legal action. Because the Catholic Church is already viewed as a rich and vulnerable organization, lawsuits in such situations are almost inevitable; the school, its owners, administrators, and teachers could face a civil negligence suit at best and criminal charges at worst. All teachers must ensure that facilities are safe and continually monitored for problem areas.

Policies should contain clear directives for dealing with threats of violence. All threats must be taken seriously, and school policies must be applied. Policies must address worst-case scenarios and ensure that appropriate procedures are in place. Each school should have a crisis management plan, and teachers must be thoroughly familiar with it and able to implement it.

SPECIFIC SAFETY PLANS

Each school should have an overall safety plan. Provisions should be made for conducting an annual safety audit, and teacher input should be sought in the development of the audit and the implementation of the plan. The requirements of all civil laws and regulations must be met. Teachers should be given a list of "do's and don'ts"; for example, adults should be instructed to refrain from chaining doors, blocking exits, and the like.

No safety plan can anticipate every possible hazard or situation that might arise, but all responsible for Catholic education have a duty to protect students, faculty, staff, and parents. Safety is one issue to which a defense of "It wasn't my job" will not be honored. Catholic school educators are held to high legal standards and, perhaps more important, to gospel standards.

A Final Thought

The ministry of Catholic education is a sacred trust. Catholic school teachers are not only professional employees, but are also ministers of the Catholic faith as well. The call to prayerful, professional service abounds in various documents of the church. Jesus once observed, "Render unto Caesar the things that are Caesar's, and unto God the things that are God's." A Catholic school teacher must constantly reflect on both legal and gospel imperatives and must attempt to meet the demands of both.

Glossary of Terms

Common Law
Common law is that law not created by a legislature. It includes principles of action based on long-established standards of reasonable conduct and on court judgments affirming such standards. It is sometimes called judge-made law.

Compelling State Interest
Compelling state interest is the overwhelming or serious need for governmental action. The government is said to have a compelling state interest in antidiscrimination legislation and in the elimination of unequal treatment of citizens.

Contract
A contract is an agreement between two parties. The essentials of a contract are: (1) mutual assent (2) by legally competent parties (3) for consideration (4) to subject matter that is legal and (5) is stated in a form prescribed by law.

Defamation
Defamation is an unprivileged communication. It can be either spoken (slander) or written (libel).

Due Process (constitutional)
Due process is fundamental fairness under the law. There are two types:

Substantive Due Process: "The constitutional guarantee that no person shall be arbitrarily deprived of his life, liberty, or property; the essence of substantive due process is protection from arbitrary unreasonable action" (Black). Substantive due process concerns *what* is done as distinguished from *how* it is done (procedural due process).

Procedural Due Process: how the process of depriving someone of something is carried out; *how it is done.* The minimum requirements of constitutional due process are *notice* and a *hearing* before an *impartial tribunal.*

Foreseeability
Foreseeability is "the reasonable anticipation that harm or injury is the likely result of acts or omission" (Black). It is not necessary that a person anticipate the particular injury that might result from an action, but only that danger or harm in general might result.

Negligence
Negligence is the absence of the degree of care which a reasonable person would be expected to use in a given situation. Legal negligence requires the presence of four elements: duty, violation of duty, proximate cause, and injury.

Proximate Cause
Proximate cause is a contributing factor to an injury. The injury was the result of a reasonably foreseeable outcome of the action or inaction said to be the proximate cause.

State Action
State action is the presence of the government in an activity to such a degree that the activity may be considered to be that of the government.

Tort
A tort is a civil or private wrong as distinguished from a crime.

Bibliography

Bischoff v. Brothers of the Sacred Heart, La. App. 416 So.2d 348 (1982).

Black, Henry Campbell. *Black's Law Dictionary* (5th ed.) (St. Paul, Minn.: West, 1979).

Brooks v. Logan School and Joint District No. 2, 903 P.2d 3 (1995).

The Buckley Amendment of 1975.

Dixon v. Alabama, 186 F.Supp. 945 (1960); reversed at 294 F.2d 150 (USCA Fifth Circuit, 1961); cert. den. 368 U.S. 930 (1961).

Dolter v. Wahlert, 483 F.Supp. 266 (N.D. Iowa 1980).

Geraci v. St. Xavier High School, 12 Ohio Op. 3d 146 (Ohio, 1978).

Individuals with Disabilities in Education Act (IDEA) Amendments (1997).

Ingraham v. Wright, 430 U.S. 65 (1977).

Levandowski v. Jackson City School District, 328 S.2d 339 (Minn. 1976).

New Jersey v. T.L.O., 105 S. Ct. 733 (1985).

NLRB v. Catholic Bishop of Chicago, 440 U.S. 490 (1979).

Pastoral Statement of U.S. Catholic Bishops on Handicapped People (1988).

Rendell-Baker v. Kohn, 102 S.Ct. 2764 (1982).

Smith v. Archbishop of St. Louis, 632 S.W.2d 516 (1982).

Tinker v. Des Moines Independent Community School District et al., 393 U.S. 503 (1969).

Titus v. Lindberg, 228 A.2d 65 (N.J., 1967).